DAILY GRATITUDE JOURNAL

Megan Gallagher
& Karen Tui Boyes

Published by Spectrum Education Limited
Lower Hutt, New Zealand
info@spectrumeducation.com

ISBN 978-1-0670169-5-1

Copyright © Spectrum Education 2024
© Karen Tui Boyes 2024
© Megan Gallagher 2024

Designed and typeset by Spectrum Education, New Zealand
Graphics & photos from Canva

All rights reserved. No part of this publication may be reproduced, stored in a retrieval system, or transmitted in any form or by any means (electronic, mechanical, photocopying or otherwise), without the prior written permission of both the copyright owner and the publisher of this book.

Welcome to Your Daily Gratitude Journey

We're so glad you've chosen to embark on this transformative journey with us!

Gratitude is a powerful practice that can shift your perspective, boost your well-being, and enrich your life in countless ways. Whether you're new to gratitude or have been practising it for years, this journal is designed to guide and support you as you explore the many facets of thankfulness.

Inside these pages, you'll find space for daily reflection, intentions, and affirmations to help you cultivate gratitude even on the tough days. The benefits of gratitude are immense—from enhancing physical health and psychological well-being to deepening social connections—and the beauty lies in its simplicity. It's not about grand gestures but about noticing the small, often overlooked moments that bring joy and meaning to our lives.

We encourage you to start each day with an open heart and mind, ready to appreciate the good around you, and to use the tools we've included to deepen your practice. This is a space for growth, self-awareness, and reflection—an opportunity to nourish your mind, body, and soul.

As you turn the pages, remember that this is your personal journey. Go at your own pace, reflect honestly, and most importantly, celebrate every step forward, no matter how small. And if ever you stumble, remember that gratitude is always within reach, waiting to offer its gifts.

Here's to finding joy in the everyday and making gratitude a lifelong habit!

with rainbows and sunshine

Karen & Meg

The Art & Science of Gratitude

Gratitude is both an art and a science, centred around the simple yet profound act of being thankful. It involves nurturing an appreciation for what we have and spreading kindness to those around us. Scientific research supports the numerous benefits of gratitude, revealing that it not only enhances our well-being and happiness but also brings substantial health benefits.

Benefits of Gratitude

- *Physical Health:* Engaging in gratitude can bolster the immune system, reduce blood pressure, and lead to better sleep, contributing to overall physical health.
- *Psychological Well-being:* It fosters an increase in positive emotions, boosts optimism, and strengthens resilience, helping us to maintain a positive outlook on life.
- *Social Life:* Practicing gratitude encourages behaviours like compassion and generosity, and it enhances our ability to connect with others, enriching our social interactions.

Ways to Cultivate Gratitude

Gratitude can be cultivated through various practices:

- Writing thank-you notes to express appreciation directly boosts both the giver's and the receiver's mood.
- Maintaining a gratitude journal helps recognise and value the positive aspects of life.
- Engaging in mindfulness and meditation focuses the mind on present blessings.
- Daily counting of blessings ingrains a habit of noticing and appreciating the good.

Gratitude on the Hard Days

Even on challenging days, gratitude has the power to shift our focus from negative to positive. It broadens our perspective, helping us find value in tough situations by:

- Making gratitude lists to visualise the positives
- Finding beneficial aspects in challenges
- Appreciating the small, often overlooked moments of joy.

The Secret of Gratitude

The true secret to unlocking the power of gratitude lies in its regular practice. By choosing to engage in gratitude daily.

- The benefits may not be immediate, they accumulate and compound over time.
- Visual reminders and the support of a community can enhance the practice and make it more effective.

How To Use Your Gratitude Journal

Intention

Setting your intention helps you to look at the week in advance and how you want to show up in the world for that week.

Intentions are a powerful way to live a big, juicy life and we have provided a space each week to do this.

Consider writing some kick-arse goals for the week. Perhaps you could record an affirmation or quote for the week. You might plan your week in advance with the following:

- 3 yummy things I will do for myself
- This week I plan to _____ and how I will feel when I have done this/met my goals for the week
- What are the three things I need to do this week to have a professionally exceptional week?
- What are the three things I need to do this week to have a personally exceptional week?

Spaces for each day

- Record three things you are grateful for each day. (You can do more than 3!)
- To up-level your gratitude, add a 'because...'
- Each day before you write your next gratitude, read what you wrote the previous day.

Reflection

Reflecting is also important and we have included a space at the end of each week for reflection. It may be helpful to use some of the suggestions below and on the next page such as the AEIOUY, the 'more of' or the reflection questions. Choose an idea and test it out for a month or two.

- In your reflection, you might give your week a mark out of 10 and record what you might do to keep things great or make it better next week
- You could write a list of challenges and wins for the week
- Another idea is to use the triple 'A's as a framework
  - What have you **A**ppreciated?
  - What do you need to **A**pologise for or put right?
  - What is an **A**-ha for you? What have you learned?

Ideas for Reflection

Just like practicing daily gratitude helps you cumulatively so does regular reflection. You may just think or you might jot your thoughts down. It can help you build greater self awareness, improve decision making and support your growth.

Reflect on your gratitude
Read what you have been grateful for over the week.
You might jot down notes about what you notice as you reflect on your week.
- What are you grateful for?
- How does gratitude make you feel?
- What impact has gratitude had on your life this week?

Focus word
A focus word acts as a guiding light, helping you stay aligned with your goals and intentions. If you have a focus word for the week, month or year you can use the space to reflect on how you lived your focus word each day. You can take the same actions reflecting on your personal values as well.

More of, Less of, Rid of, Toss in
You might like to reflect on your week and then write a list for the next week:
- More of- what you would like more of
- Less of- what you would like less of
- Rid of- what you would like to get rid of
- Toss in- what you would like to toss in or add to your day

AEIOUY
Brené Brown's AEIOUY can be a useful tool. Reflect of one thing for each of the following for the day or week:
- A = Abstain- what you abstained from
- E = Exercise- how you moved your body
- I = Me, myself and I- what you did for yourself
- O = Others - what you did for others
- U = Unsaid- what you left unsaid
- Y = YAY!- what has been a success for you

Questions
Answer the following questions:
- What went well today?
- What is one thing you would you do differently if you could repeat this day?
- What have you learned?

About Us

Karen's Gratitude Journey

Gratitude has been a central part of my life, nurtured from childhood by my Dad's belief that "every day's a good day," a mindset that balanced out my Mum's high expectations. As a child I was inspired by the story of Pollyanna and her "glad game," where she found joy in small things and vividly recall the rainbows created by crystal pendants hanging from a lamp.

Over the years, I've always been a positive thinker, believing in luck, the power of intention, and the importance of helping others succeed. Six years ago, I began a formal gratitude practice by starting the Daily Gratitude Practice Facebook Group, initially sparked by a friend's negativity. I invited people to share three things they were grateful for each day for 30 days. While my friend didn't participate, 40 of my other friends did, and after the first month, they insisted on keeping the group going. Today, the group has grown to over 900 members.

Sharing this practice publicly deepened my own experience and accountability and led me to run several gratitude retreats, build incredible friendships, and discover the true power of gratitude. Creating this gratitude journal is a dream come true, especially as I have had the joy of collaborating on it with my best friend and work wife, Meg.

Megan's Story of Gratitude

A number of years ago I went through some dark days, that turned into dark weeks. It felt like I was at the bottom of a well and the only light I could see seemed so very far away. Despite the sense of hopelessness I knew that in order to get out of this dark place I needed help. One of the tools I found was gratitude.

Every night I would write a list of things I was grateful for, and every morning I would read what I had written the night before. At first it was so damned hard to find the gratitude and as the days passed I noticed it becoming easier. I also found that what I was grateful for became more personally meaningful.

This has since become a part of my life and something I share with my family. One tradition we now have is we talk about what we are grateful for around the dinner table. I am so grateful for all the adventures I have with Karen including this book.

__/__/__

Intention

Monday

Tuesday

Wednesday

Thursday

Friday

Saturday

Sunday

"Gratitude is the healthiest of all human emotions."
- Zig Ziglar

Reflection

__/__/__

Intention

Monday

Tuesday

Wednesday

Thursday

Friday

Saturday

Sunday

"Gratitude is a powerful force that can transform your life."
- Oprah Winfrey

Reflection

__/__/__

Intention

Monday

Tuesday

Wednesday

Thursday

Friday

Saturday

Sunday

"Gratitude is the inward feeling of kindness received. Thankfulness is the natural impulse to express that feeling."
- Henry Van Dyke

Reflection

__/__/__

Intention

Monday

Tuesday

Wednesday

Thursday

Friday

Saturday

Sunday

"Gratitude is the memory of the heart."
- Jean-Baptiste Massieu

Reflection

__/__/__

Intention

Monday

Tuesday

Wednesday

Thursday

Friday

Saturday

Sunday

"Gratitude is the ability to experience life as a gift. It liberates us from the prison of self-preoccupation."
- John Ortberg

Reflection

__/__/__

Intention

Monday

Tuesday

Wednesday

Thursday

Friday

Saturday

Sunday

"Gratitude is a powerful catalyst for a meaningful life. It opens the door to the beauty of the present moment."
- M.J. Ryan

Reflection

__/__/__

Intention

Monday

Tuesday

Wednesday

Thursday

Friday

Saturday

Sunday

"The essence of all beautiful art is gratitude."
- Friedrich Nietzsche

Reflection

__/__/__

Intention

Monday

Tuesday

Wednesday

Thursday

Friday

Saturday

Sunday

"Gratitude is the completion of thankfulness. Thankfulness may consist merely of words. Gratitude is shown in acts."
- Henri Frederic Amiel

Reflection

__/__/__

Intention

Monday

Tuesday

Wednesday

Thursday

Friday

Saturday

Sunday

"Gratitude paints little smiley faces on everything it touches."
- Richelle E. Goodrich

Reflection

__/__/__

Intention

Monday

Tuesday

Wednesday

Thursday

Friday

Saturday

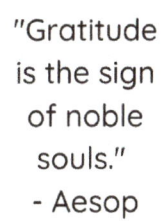

Sunday

"Gratitude is the sign of noble souls."
- Aesop

Reflection

__/__/__

Intention

Monday

Tuesday

Wednesday

Thursday

Friday

Saturday

Sunday

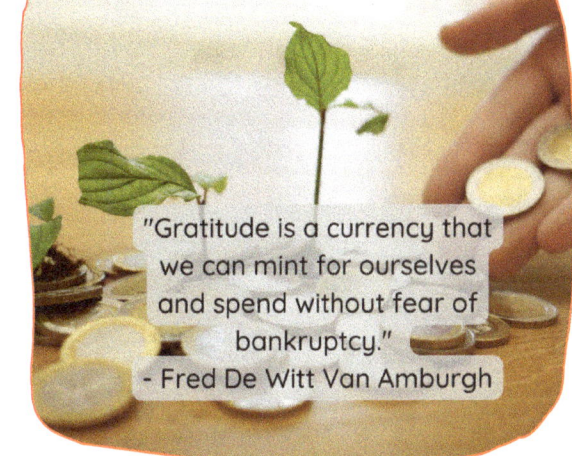

"Gratitude is a currency that we can mint for ourselves and spend without fear of bankruptcy."
- Fred De Witt Van Amburgh

Reflection

__/__/__

Intention

Monday

Tuesday

Wednesday

Thursday

Friday

Saturday

Sunday

"Gratitude is a powerful catalyst for happiness. It's the spark that lights a fire of joy in your soul."
- Amy Collette

Reflection

__/__/__

Intention

Monday

Tuesday

Wednesday

Thursday

Friday

Saturday

Sunday

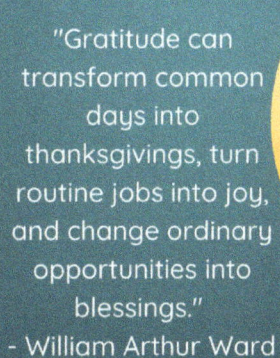

"Gratitude can transform common days into thanksgivings, turn routine jobs into joy, and change ordinary opportunities into blessings."
— William Arthur Ward

Reflection

__/__/__

Intention

Monday

Tuesday

Wednesday

Thursday

Friday

Saturday

Sunday

"Gratitude is the music of the heart, when its chords are swept by the breeze of kindness."
- Unknown

Reflection

__/__/__

Intention

Monday

Tuesday

Wednesday

Thursday

Friday

Saturday

Sunday

"Gratitude is the fairest blossom which springs from the soul."
- Henry Ward Beecher

Reflection

__/__/__

Intention

Monday

Tuesday

Wednesday

Thursday

Friday

Saturday

Sunday

"Gratitude is the wine for the soul. Go on. Get drunk."
- Rumi

Reflection

__/__/__

Intention

Monday

Tuesday

Wednesday

Thursday

Friday

Saturday

Sunday

> "Gratitude is the sweetest thing in a seeker's life."
> - Sri Chinmoy

Reflection

__/__/__

Intention

Monday

Tuesday

Wednesday

Thursday

Friday

Saturday

Sunday

"Gratitude is a quality similar to electricity: it must be produced and discharged and used up in order to exist at all."
— William Faulkner

Reflection

__/__/__

Intention

Monday

Tuesday

Wednesday

Thursday

Friday

Saturday

Sunday

"The more grateful I am, the more beauty I see."
- Mary Davis

Reflection

__/__/__

Intention

Monday

Tuesday

Wednesday

Thursday

Friday

Saturday

Sunday

"When you are grateful, fear disappears and abundance appears."
- Tony Robbins

Reflection

__/__/__

Intention

Monday

Tuesday

Wednesday

Thursday

Friday

Saturday

Sunday

"The root of joy is gratefulness."
- David Steindl-Rast

Reflection

__/__/__

Intention

Monday

Tuesday

Wednesday

Thursday

Friday

Saturday

Sunday

"Feeling gratitude and not expressing it is like wrapping a present and not giving it."
— William Arthur Ward

Reflection

__/__/__

Intention

Monday

Tuesday

Wednesday

Thursday

Friday

Saturday

Sunday

"Gratitude makes sense of our past, brings peace for today, and creates a vision for tomorrow."
- Melody Beattie

Reflection

__/__/__

Intention

Monday

Tuesday

Wednesday

Thursday

Friday

Saturday

Sunday

"Gratitude is not only the greatest of virtues but the parent of all others."
- Marcus Tullius Cicero

Reflection

__/__/__

Intention

Monday

Tuesday

Wednesday

Thursday

Friday

Saturday

Sunday

"In ordinary life, we hardly realize that we receive a great deal more than we give, and that it is only with gratitude that life becomes rich."
- Dietrich Bonhoeffer

Reflection

__/__/__

Intention

Monday

Tuesday

Wednesday

Thursday

Friday

Saturday

Sunday

"Gratitude is when memory is stored in the heart and not in the mind."
- Lionel Hampton

Reflection

__/__/__

Intention

Monday

Tuesday

Wednesday

Thursday

Friday

Saturday

Sunday

"Acknowledging the good that you already have in your life is the foundation for all abundance."
- Eckhart Tolle

Reflection

__/__/__

Intention

Monday

Tuesday

Wednesday

Thursday

Friday

Saturday

Sunday

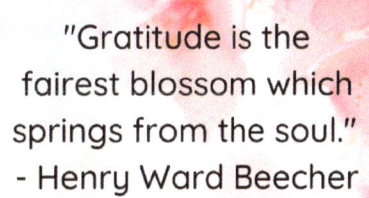

"Gratitude is the fairest blossom which springs from the soul."
- Henry Ward Beecher

Reflection

__/__/__

Intention

Monday

Tuesday

Wednesday

Thursday

Friday

Saturday

Sunday

"Gratitude unlocks the fullness of life."
- Melody Beattie

Reflection

__/__/__

Intention

Monday

Tuesday

Wednesday

Thursday

Friday

Saturday

Sunday

> "Gratitude turns what we have into enough."
> - Anonymous

Reflection

__/__/__

Intention

Monday

Tuesday

Wednesday

Thursday

Friday

Saturday

Sunday

> "It's a funny thing about life, once you begin to take note of the things you are grateful for, you begin to lose sight of the things that you lack."
> -Germany Kent

Reflection

__/__/__

Intention

Monday

Tuesday

Wednesday

Thursday

Friday

Saturday

Sunday

"Gratitude helps you fall in love with the life you already have."
- Kristen Hewitt

Reflection

__/__/__

Intention

Monday

Tuesday

Wednesday

Thursday

Friday

Saturday

Sunday

"Gratitude is the antidote to bitterness and resentment."
- Marianne Williamson

Reflection

__/__/__

Intention

Monday

Tuesday

Wednesday

Thursday

Friday

Saturday

Sunday

"Gratitude and attitude are not challenges; they are choices."
- Robert Braathe

Reflection

__/__/__

Intention

Monday

Tuesday

Wednesday

Thursday

Friday

Saturday

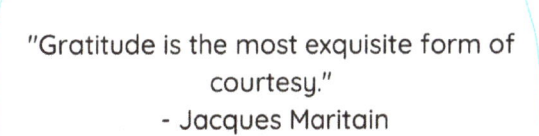

Sunday

> "Gratitude is the most exquisite form of courtesy."
> - Jacques Maritain

Reflection

__/__/__

Intention

Monday

Tuesday

Wednesday

Thursday

Friday

Saturday

Sunday

"God gave you a gift of 86,400 seconds today. Have you used one to say thank you?"
- William Arthur Ward

Reflection

__/__/__

Intention

Monday

Tuesday

Wednesday

Thursday

Friday

Saturday

Sunday

"Enjoy the little things, for one day you may look back and realize they were the big things."
- Robert Brault

Reflection

__/__/__

Intention

Monday

Tuesday

Wednesday

Thursday

Friday

Saturday

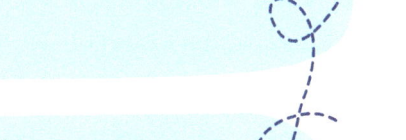

Sunday

"When we focus on our gratitude, the tide of disappointment goes out and the tide of love rushes in."
- Kristin Armstrong

Reflection

__/__/__

Intention

Monday

Tuesday

Wednesday

Thursday

Friday

Saturday

Sunday

"This is a wonderful day. I have never seen this one before."
- Maya Angelou

Reflection

__/__/__

Intention

Monday

Tuesday

Wednesday

Thursday

Friday

Saturday

Sunday

"Gratitude is the bridge to happiness."
— Anonymous

Reflection

__/__/__

Intention

Monday

Tuesday

Wednesday

Thursday

Friday

Saturday

Sunday

"Gratitude is the most exquisite form of courtesy."
- Jacques Maritain

Reflection

__/__/__

Intention

Monday

Tuesday

Wednesday

Thursday

Friday

Saturday

Sunday

"Gratitude is the secret to seeing life's magic."
- Anonymous

Reflection

__/__/__

Intention

Monday

Tuesday

Wednesday

Thursday

Friday

Saturday

Sunday

"Let us be grateful to people who make us happy; they are the charming gardeners who make our souls blossom."
-Marcel Proust

Reflection

__/__/__

Intention

Monday

Tuesday

Wednesday

Thursday

Friday

Saturday

Sunday

"No duty is more urgent than giving thanks."
- James Allen

Reflection

__/__/__

Intention

Monday

Tuesday

Wednesday

Thursday

Friday

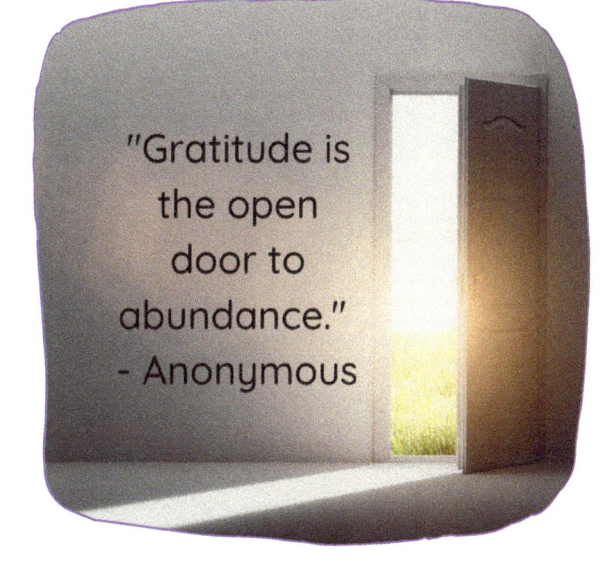

Saturday

Sunday

"Gratitude is the open door to abundance."
- Anonymous

Reflection

__/__/__

Intention

Monday

Tuesday

Wednesday

Thursday

Friday

Saturday

Sunday

"Let us be grateful to the mirror for revealing to us our appearance only."
- Samuel Butler

Reflection

__/__/__

Intention

Monday

Tuesday

Wednesday

Thursday

Friday

Saturday

Sunday

> "The deepest craving of human nature is the need to be appreciated."
> - William James

Reflection

__/__/__

Intention

Monday

Tuesday

Wednesday

Thursday

Friday

Saturday

Sunday

"Gratitude is the seed of abundance."
- Anonymous

Reflection

__/__/__

Intention

Monday

Tuesday

Wednesday

Thursday

Friday

Saturday

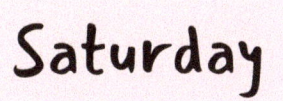

Sunday

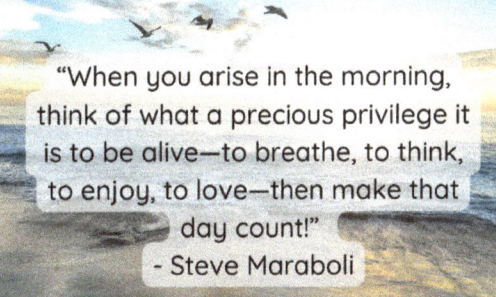

"When you arise in the morning, think of what a precious privilege it is to be alive—to breathe, to think, to enjoy, to love—then make that day count!"
- Steve Maraboli

Reflection

__/__/__

Intention

Monday

Tuesday

Wednesday

Thursday

Friday

Saturday

Sunday

"The power of finding beauty in the humblest things makes home happy and life lovely."
- Louisa May Alcott

Reflection

__/__/__

Intention

Monday

Tuesday

Wednesday

Thursday

Friday

Saturday

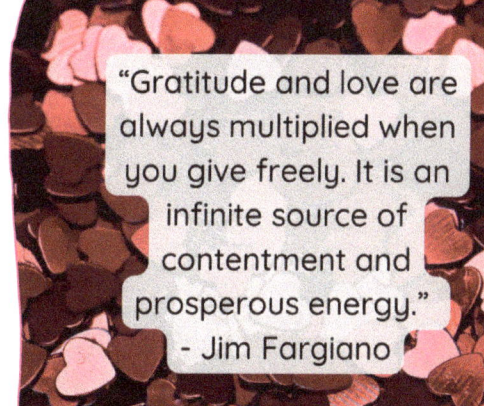

Sunday

"Gratitude and love are always multiplied when you give freely. It is an infinite source of contentment and prosperous energy."
- Jim Fargiano

Reflection

__/__/__

Intention

Monday

Tuesday

Wednesday

Thursday

Friday

Saturday

Sunday

"Life is a web of intersections and choices. Your 1st choice is to recognize an intersection. Your 2nd choice is to be grateful for it."
- Ryan Lilly

Reflection

Meg & Karen's Books and Courses

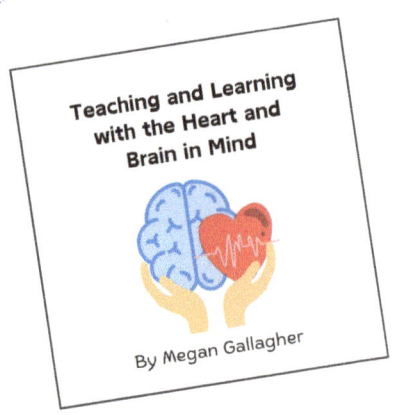

Teaching and Learning with the Heart and Brain in Mind is a powerful guide for educators seeking to transform their classrooms and themselves. Drawing from personal experiences, emotional literacy, neuroscience, and psychology, Megan Gallagher offers practical strategies to manage stress, improve relationships with learners, and create a learning environment that truly nurtures both heart and mind.

ONLINE COURSE: Happy Healthy Teachers Matter — 10-4 Challenge

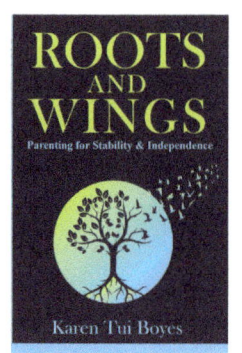

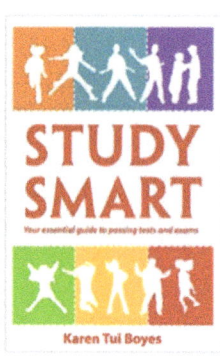

Sample topics — *Find out more*

- Energy flows where attention goes
- Get curious not furious
- Automate some decisions / Reduce decision fatigue
- Just one step at a time

Books by Karen Tui Boyes

- A Taste of Gratitude — Delicious Dishes & Positive Vibes
- Creating the Life of Your Dreams — A step by step guide to vision boarding
- Project Genius — BIG Learning for Small Geniuses
- Roots and Wings — Parenting for Stability & Independence
- Study Smart — Your essential guide to passing tests and exams

Find out more at **www.spectrumeducation.com**

Meg & Karen's Blogs

www.meggallagher.nz/blog

www.spectrumeducation.com/karens-articles-blog/

Our Contact Details

Megan and Karen are available for conference keynote, workshop speaking and in-service professional development

Megan Gallagher
www.meggallagher.nz
meg@meggallagher.nz

Karen Tui Boyes
www.spectrumeducation.com
karen@spectrumeducation.com